foundations

Seven group studies to
introduce the essentials
of Christian living

JOHN GROVES

NEWFRONTIERS USA
SAINT LOUIS, MISSOURI USA

First published by King's Church, Hastings 2002
and by Kingsway 2007
This new edition published by Newfrontiers USA 2008

ISBN 978-0-9814803-0-5

Cover design by Jodi Hertz
Typesetting by PinnacleCreative.co.uk

Published by
NEWFRONTIERS USA
P.O. Box 2626, Saint Louis, MO 63116 USA
email: office@newfrontiers-usa.org
Printed in the United States

Contents

UNIT 1
Personal Foundations

Day 1   The Peter Package   6
Day 2   Repentance   8
Day 3   Faith   10
Day 4   Baptism In Water   12
Day 5   Baptism In The Holy Spirit   15

UNIT 2
A New Creation

Day 1   A Fresh Start   20
Day 2   A Son Of God   22
Day 3   Not Under Law   24
Day 4   Grace Rules!   26
Day 5   Winning, Not Sinning   28

UNIT 3
Kingdom Life

Day 1   The Kingdom Of God   32
Day 2   Kingdom Life – Personal   34
Day 3   Kingdom Life – Family   36
Day 4   Kingdom Life – Work   38
Day 5   Kingdom Life – The World   40

UNIT 4
Kingdom Warfare

Day 1   Know The Enemy   44
Day 2   The Enemy's Strategy   46
Day 3   Jesus Has Overcome Satan   48
Day 4   How We Overcome Satan   50
Day 5   Your Armour And Weapons   52

UNIT 5
Jesus Is Building His Church

Day 1   What Is The Church? (Pt.1)   56
Day 2   What Is The Church? (Pt.2)   58
Day 3   Which Church?   60
Day 4   A Worshipping Church   62
Day 5   A Member Of The Body   64

UNIT 6
Belonging To A Church

Day 1   A Healthy Church (Pt.1)   68
Day 2   A Healthy Church (Pt.2)   70
Day 3   Leadership   72
Day 4   Stewardship (Pt.1)   74
Day 5   Stewardship (Pt.2)   76

UNIT 7
Sharing Your Faith

Day 1   You Will Be My Witnesses   78
Day 2   Actions Speak!   80
Day 3   Leading Someone To Christ   81
Day 4   Signs And Wonders   83
Day 5   To The Ends Of The Earth   85

How to use the course

Foundations is a course designed to introduce you to some of the foundational beliefs of our Church. It has the additional purpose of ensuring that your own personal Christian foundations are strong and healthy.

The course lasts for eight weeks and is divided into seven units. Each unit is sub-divided into five sections, which can be done on your own on five separate days during the week before the group meeting.

You will need approximately twenty minutes for each study. Then, when you come to the group meeting, we can cover some of the main teachings, confident that you have a knowledge of the subject. It also means that you can have thought over questions which you may want to ask the course leaders.

An additional benefit of the Foundations Course is that it gives the leaders of the church a chance to get to know you and for you to get to know them.

The first evening will serve as an introduction to ourselves and to the first unit, 'Personal Foundations'. During the week following this, we would ask you to do the five personal studies of Unit 1, in preparation for further discussion in the second week's group meeting.

At the end of the course there will be opportunity for you to speak to the leaders privately. Please feel free to ask for prayer or to bring up more sensitive issues then.

An additional benefit of the course being in this format is that it can be used for one-to-one discipleship. Each week the person being discipled should do the five studies that make up the unit. Then when he or she meets with their discipler they can go through the studies, ensure everything is understood and deal with any questions raised by the studies.

The New International Version of the Bible has been used for all the Bible references.

PERSONAL FOUNDATIONS

The Peter Package

Are you sitting comfortably?

A stable, strong Christian life can be likened to a good, sturdy chair! You need four legs all fixed firmly in place! If one or more of the legs is missing or loose the chair will feel wobbly and sitting on it will feel anything but secure and relaxing!

In the same way, there are four important elements to a stable, strong Christian life and what you can learn from the Bible is that all four need to be firmly in place for a healthy Christian life.

This week we want you to check that the 'four legs' of your Christian life are in place, so that you feel secure as you go about your daily life.

📖 *Read Acts 2 v 36–41.*

This is an account of the first sermon of the Church Age, our Age! Peter preaches about Jesus and when the people listening ask Him, 'What shall we do?' He gives them the answer which is in verse 38.

There are **four elements** to Peter's answer:

▪ Turn away from what you've done wrong	»	Repentance
▪ Believe in Jesus for the forgiveness of your sins	»	Faith
▪ Be baptised in water to show you have put faith in Jesus	»	Baptism in Water
▪ Receive the gift of the Holy Spirit	»	Baptism in the Spirit

As you go through the Book of Acts, you will see these four elements of the Christian experience are always there, but they aren't applied in a legalistic way and there is no mechanical formula.

Read Acts 8 v 9–17.

The people turn from following an occult magician *(v 9–13)* – **Repentance**
The people believed in Jesus *(v 12)* – **Faith**
The people were baptised in water *(v 12)* – **Baptism in Water**
The people received the gift of the Holy Spirit *(v 15 and 17)* – **Baptism in the Spirit**

 Read Acts 9 v 17–18.

Paul has already repented (turned from) his old evil ways and believed in Jesus *(see v 1–6)*. Here, he is filled with the Holy Spirit and baptised in water.

Is the order of these events the same as with the Samaritans in Acts 8?
Yes ☐ No ☐

 Read Acts 19 v 1–7.

This is the start of the church in the city of Ephesus. When Paul first visits the city he finds some God-fearing people but he is concerned that something is missing.

They clearly didn't have four legs to their chair!

Write out the question Paul asks them in v 2.

_____

_____

Does this question imply that it is possible to believe in Jesus and not yet have received the empowering of the Holy Spirit?
Yes ☐ No ☐

What was the 'ONE LEG' that these people had?
Repentance ☐ Baptism ☐

Notice Paul explains putting faith in Jesus and they are now baptised AGAIN *(see verses 4 and 5)*. Only, it's not really AGAIN because the first baptism involved no faith in Jesus for the forgiveness of sins and a new life.

What was the final 'LEG' Paul fixed in place? (see v 6).

_____

Repentance

Hopefully, this is something you've already done when you became a Christian. However, to have a firm foundation in your Christian life, you need to understand this very important element.

The word **'REPENT'** in the Bible implies movement. It means

'To turn from'   or **'To return to'**

When you **'REPENT'** you realise that you are going away from God and so you do a complete about turn towards God.

Fill in the missing words in this verse:

In the past God overlooked such ignorance, but now He _____

all people everywhere to_____. *(Acts 17 v 30).*

To repent is a personal decision.

> I recognise that God is wholly right
> and that I am wholly wrong

Read Romans 3 v 23 and Isaiah 55 v 8–9.

> I see that I need a change of mind and a change of heart
> as well as a change of direction

To repent is a practical step – it involves zeal and action.

Read 2 Corinthians 7 v 10–11.

> I **stop** doing ungodly things and **start** doing godly things

In Luke 3 v 8 we are told '**Produce fruit** in keeping with repentance'.

📖 *Now look at Luke 3 v 10–14.*

✏️ *Write down FOUR examples of changes as a result of repentance.*

1. _____

2. _____

3. _____

4. _____

In other parts of the New Testament we see people who repent,

» getting rid of their idols

» burning occult books

» paying back money they had stolen

! Can you THINK of **radical changes** you went through when you became a Christian? Ask God if there are areas He wants you to put right in your life at this time. If there are – do something about it!

```
Important Notice!
```

2 Corinthians 7 v 10–11 refers to people who were already Christians having to repent of things they have done wrong.

```
Repentance is NOT just something you do ONCE
at the beginning of your Christian life.
```

Many believers need to 'clear themselves' as the Corinthians had to.

Be open to God speaking to you.

Faith

Faith is the basis of our relationship with God from the start.

 **Read Hebrews 11 v 6.**

Faith does not get its certainty from the realm of our physical senses or our emotions.

Read Hebrews 11 v 1.

Faith comes from accepting what God says in His Word.

Read Romans 10 v 17.

a) We Are Saved By Faith

John 3 v 16 and Mark 16 v 16 make it very clear that we are saved by believing what God has said about Jesus Christ His Son.

We	**BELIEVE**	that Jesus is the Son of God sent by the Father as the only way of salvation *(Acts 4 v 12)*
We	**TRUST**	wholly and only in Jesus and His death on the cross to save us from our sins *(Romans 3 v 22-24)*
We	**CONFESS**	that Jesus is alive and is the Lord of our lives *(Romans 10 v 9-10)*
We	**RECEIVE**	from God the gift of eternal life *(John 3 v 36)*

b) We Are Justified By Faith

Justification is a picture from the law courts. A person is justified if they are declared legally innocent for a crime they were once pronounced guilty of.

In our case, we **WERE** guilty of our sins before the court of a holy God. However, Jesus bore the punishment due to us. My sins have been **PAID FOR** and are, therefore, legally removed. I can be righteous or 'in right standing' with a holy God.

This is the gospel God has announced and my faith in this message means I can be justified. Faith in Jesus is the ONLY WAY that I can be justified.

📖 *Read Romans 3 v 21–26 and Romans 5 v 6–11.*

Read these passages carefully and ask God to help you understand them. Then THANK GOD for what He has done for you through Jesus His Son.

c) We Walk By Faith

The Christian life is a life of faith.

The key Biblical example of faith is Abraham. When Paul wanted to illustrate faith he recounted Abraham's relationship with God. The manner in which Abraham manifested faith is the manner in which we must manifest faith.

📖 *Read Romans 4 v 13–21.*

» He heard the word of God and believed what God had promised him *(v 13 and v 21)*.

» He did not consider his own abilities as the determining factor *(v 19)*.

» He embraced the hope expressed in the divine promise *(v 18)*.

» He did not waver in his commitment to God's word *(v 20)*.

» He gave glory to God out of His faith in God, even before he saw the full accomplishment of the promise *(v 20–21)*.

Baptism in Water

There is confusion and controversy among Christians about **water baptism.** We need to be clear as to what the Bible teaches. There is no confusion or uncertainty about it if we rely on Scripture alone. It tells us how baptism is to be practised and what it really means.

a) It Is For Believers

Baptism in Scripture always follows repentance and faith.
(e.g. *Mark 16 v 16; Acts 2 v 38*).

It was after a person became a disciple that he or she was to be baptised. (*Matthew 28 v 19*).

We never find the order reversed. Check all the Acts incidents of baptism and you will find, even with the Philippian jailer's family (*Acts 16 v 31–34*), that **repentance and faith preceded baptism.**

There is no age limit for baptism. However, the youngest person who is baptised is expected to know Jesus as their Saviour, be willing to obey Him as Lord and have some understanding of turning from their sins.

b) It Is By Immersion

The Greek word for baptise means 'to dip; to immerse; to submerge'. New Testament believers were, therefore, immersed in water. So John needed plenty of water to do the job (*John 3 v 23*). This is confirmed by the description of Jesus' baptism (*Mark 1 v 10*). Also, with Philip and the Eunuch (*Acts 8 v 38–39*).

c) What Does It Mean?

The moment you became a Christian, your life was linked with Jesus Christ, you were baptised (immersed) into Him and what happened to Him happened to you as well. You **died with Him** to sin and to its power over you. And you **rose with Him** to a brand new life. When you are baptised you are **identifying** with Him.

📖 *Read Romans 6 v 3–7.*

✍️ *Write down the answers to the following questions.*

Who are we baptised into? *(v 3)* _____

What are we baptised into? *(v 3)* _____

Which part of us has been crucified? *(v 6)* _____

Why does it need to die? *(v 7)* _____

What are we now able to do? *(v 4)* _____

When you **go down** in the water you are saying:

'Lord Jesus, You died on the cross for me.
From now on, my old life is dead. I've broken with sin.'

When you are **under** the water you are saying:

'Lord, just as You were buried in the tomb, so my old sinful life is
now buried in the water. This baptism is my funeral.'

When you are **lifted out** of the water you are saying:

'Lord, You were raised from the dead by God's power,
and by that power I can now live a totally new life.'

> **To Think About!**

📖 *Read Matthew 28 v 19–20.*

✍️ *Does Jesus want new Christians to be baptised?*

_____

Read Acts 10 v 48.

Do you think that new Christians should be baptised even if they don't feel like it?

You may not have been baptised as a believer because it would have been really costly for you and you wondered if you could go through with it. Remember what Jesus did for you. He actually DIED for you and identified completely with your sin. He wants you to identify with Him and confess openly:

**'I'm in Christ! My old life is dead and buried. From now on,
Jesus is my Lord and I'm living for Him.'**

Jesus has done more for you than He is ever asking you to do for Him.

*If you haven't been baptised as a believer talk this through
with the person taking you through this course.*

Baptism In The Holy Spirit

From the very beginning of your Christian life, the Holy Spirit has been working in you. You are 'Born again' by the Holy Spirit. However, Jesus promised the disciples that they would receive a dynamic power to witness for Him when the Holy Spirit came upon them *(Acts 1 v 4-8)*.

📖 ***Read Acts 2 v 38-39.***

✍ ***Was the promise of the Spirit only meant for the New Testament believers or does it apply to you too?*** (See *v 39*).

_____

When Paul met 'disciples' at Ephesus *(Acts 19 v 1-7)* he felt something lacking and asked a very basic question.

'Did you receive the Holy Spirit when you believed?'

He knew that there was a receiving of the gift of the Holy Spirit which every believer was entitled to, but not every believer had automatically. He also expected them to know whether they had been filled with the Holy Spirit or not.

To Think About !

📖 ***Read Acts 2 v 1-4.***   📖 ***Read Acts 8 v 12-17.***
📖 ***Read Acts 10 v 44-48.***   📖 ***Read Acts 19 v 1-7.***

✍ ***According to these accounts, is the baptism in the Spirit a definite experience? i.e. would you know if you'd had it?***

_____

_____

From these verses, find out what you can about how people knew Christians were filled with the Holy Spirit and write your answers below.

_____

_____

_____

Look at the following verses and write down what Jesus promised that the Holy Spirit would do for us.

Read John 14 v 26. _____

Read John 15 v 26. _____

Read John 16 v 8. _____

Read John 16 v 13. _____

Read John 16 v 14. _____

How To Receive The Baptism In The Holy Spirit

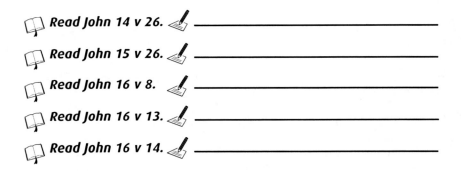

Read John 1 v 29 and v 33

Who is the one who baptises us in the Holy Spirit?

_____

Jesus told us the right way to receive

Read John 7 v 37–39

'If anyone is thirsty' – a deep longing for God to meet you in this way is essential for receiving the Holy Spirit. If you are not thirsty ask God why!

'Come to me' – go to Jesus and ask. God gives to those who ask. *(see Luke 11 v 13).*

'Drink' – drinking is an act of faith. Lay hold of the blessing. Be ready to receive.

Faith plays an important part in all this. When you come to Jesus, resist the temptation to passively wait for something to happen.

'Laying on of hands' is a ministry to help you receive. It is biblical (*Acts 8 v 17; 9 v 17; 19 v 6*) and a channel of faith for imparting the Spirit.

If you want to be prayed for to receive the baptism in the Holy Spirit, ask the person taking you through this course.

If you are not sure as to whether or not you are baptised in the Holy Spirit, please talk to a Church Leader.

NOTES

UNIT

2

A NEW CREATION

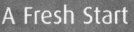

A Fresh Start

📖 **Read 2 Corinthians 5 v 17–21.**

What God has done for us IN CHRIST is amazing!

📖 **Look at 2 Corinthians 5 v 21 and then answer these questions.**

✎ Who do you think is the 'him who had no sin'? _____

✎ Our sin is put on Him. What do we get given to us?

_____

📖 **Read Colossians 2 v 13–15.**

God has 'disarmed' Satan and his demons by the cross. Basically, your sin gave Satan a legitimate hold on your life. Now your sin has been removed by being nailed to the cross with Jesus. **Satan's legal hold on your life is broken.**

The blood of Jesus, God's Son, purifies us from **ALL** sin. *(1 John 1 v 7).* Hallelujah!

God's will for us is wholeness with nothing binding us or holding us up. Jesus has set us free from the guilt and the power of sin.

This legal freedom is very real but it needs applying as a literal freedom in our daily lives. We need to **KNOW** it, **BELIEVE** it and **ACT** on it!

A large part of the battle is **KNOWING THE TRUTH** of who you are **IN CHRIST.** However, there are certain pre-conversion experiences for which we may need special help in order that we may not only enjoy legal freedom but freedom in experience. *Take this opportunity to think over any areas where you may feel oppressed or bound.*

To Consider ...

If you've been involved in certain experiences you may need help to enjoy your freedom in Christ.

Here are some examples:

OCCULT INFLUENCE
e.g. fortune telling, spiritualism, magic, witchcraft, some alternative medicines.

FALSE RELIGIONS
e.g. cults, pagan religions, extreme legalistic church life, Freemasonry, New Age religion

DRUG & ALCOHOL ABUSE

SEXUAL PERVERSION

HABITUAL GAMBLING

TRAUMATIC REJECTION

This week would be a good opportunity to pray over any problem areas, either on your own or with another mature Christian.

Please ask the person taking you through this course about any issues raised by this study.

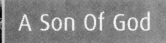

A Son Of God

'How great is the love the Father has lavished on us, that we should be called children of God! And that is what we are!' *(1 John 3 v 1).*

It is an amazing privilege to be a child of God.

📖 ***Read John 1 v 12–13*** and then answer these questions:

✍ ***How did you become a child of God?***

_____

✍ ***How are we 'born of God'?*** *(John 3 v 8 will help you).*

_____

📖 ***Read Galatians 3 v 26–27 and 4 v 4–7.***

We all become **sons of God**. This is because we share in Jesus' sonship. We are joint heirs with Him. This means your standing before God is the same whoever you are, man or woman, young or old, rich or poor. God is your Father and other Christians are members of your family. Your problems of **identity** (who you are) and **security** (where you belong) are now solved.

Being sons of God brings marvellous privileges and challenging responsibilities.

> We can be led by the Spirit of God
>
> We can be free from fear
>
> We can know God's love in our hearts
>
> We can be certain of God's acceptance of us
>
> We are co-heirs with Christ
>
> We are called to be like Jesus
>
> We receive discipline from a loving Father
>
> We receive good gifts from a loving Father

📖 *Read carefully the whole of Romans Chapter 8, paying particular attention to v 14–17 and v 28–39.*

Now THANK GOD for bringing you into His family.

Not Under Law

Fundamentally, there are only two religions in the world:

1) The religion of law
2) The religion of grace

The New Testament gospel alone is a religion of **grace.**

> Every other religion, including the Old Covenant religion of the Jews,
> is a religion of law.

LAW states *do's* and *don'ts* by which people try hard to get right with God.

The gospel of Jesus Christ does not emphasise what we have to do for God but what **He has already done for us**

📖 *Read Hebrews 7 v 18–19 and Romans 8 v 3.*

✏️ *Explain why the law was 'weak' and 'useless':*

_____

To be 'SAVED BY GRACE' means we are saved by the love-inspired actions of God, not our own efforts.

Grace is...

'SOMETHING FOR NOTHING, FOR THOSE WHO DON'T DESERVE ANYTHING.'

No man or woman has ever deserved God's mercy, so salvation had to be a gift *(Romans 6 v 23)*. We owe everything in our salvation and in our Christian life to grace *(Ephesians 2 v 8–9)*.

Grace is God's unlimited supply of mercy, love, strength, wisdom. It is, in fact, all we need flowing freely to us through Jesus Christ *(John 1 v 16–17)*.

So what is the use of the law?

 *Read Romans 7 v 7–14.*

1) The law	**reveals**	sin

We tend to live by our own standards with each individual simply acting as his or her conscience allows.

By contrast, God's law provides us with absolute standards about what is acceptable and what is not. The law is like a plumb line revealing just how crooked our lives are.

2) The law	**provokes**	sin

People are happy with a sort of 'Father Christmas' God who makes no demands. But when God reveals His holy law and tells us there are things we should and shouldn't do we get angry and rebellious. This simply proves how sinful our hearts really are.

3) The law	**leads**	us to Christ

» The law frustrates and condemns us because we simply are not good enough to keep it.

» It drives us to cry out for mercy.

» It leads us to the grace of God in Jesus Christ. We realise we have to be saved by grace if we are going to be saved at all.

Christ's death not only loosed us from our sin but also loosed us from the law.

Now we are **UNITED WITH CHRIST** and under a very different reign,

'THE REIGN OF GRACE'.

Grace Rules!

'Well then' you say, 'If I am saved by the grace of God no matter what I do, then, I can live how I like and still be saved!'.

Right ✓ and wrong ✗ !

You wouldn't be the first to say this *(Romans 3 v 8 and Romans 6 v 1)*.

It is a logical conclusion from the gospel of grace.
Technically, this position is right and accurate.

However, the other side of the coin is that, if you are **truly saved**, you are indwelt by the living presence of the Holy Spirit of God. You have also come to love and follow Jesus as you responded to His grace. A person like that simply would not calculate to live as sinfully as they could because they had got a ticket to heaven in their pocket! That attitude would prove that you didn't really know Jesus. You see, the grace of God is powerful to **change** us. Actually, grace brings **victory** that law could never bring.

📖 *Read Romans 6 v 14.*

Grace is manifested in the presence of the Holy Spirit in our lives. He is the grace of God **IN** us. He causes us to walk in a different way as He renews our minds and directs our lives.

Grace has brought us into a living, love relationship with God. Actually, we find a love for Jesus growing inside us. It's a miracle because we've never seen Him and yet we love Him!

📖 *Read Titus 2 v 11-12.*

✏️ *Write down what the grace of God teaches us.*

_____

_____

Legalism, going back to a life of rules and regulations, is one of the biggest causes of defeat and deadness amongst Christians. It means that **human effort** is taking the place of **the power of the Holy Spirit** and we are back under law.

 Read Galatians 3 v 1–5 and then answer these questions.

How do we receive the Holy Spirit? (v 2 and v 5).

_____

Having begun in the Spirit, how are the Galatians now trying to live? (v 3).

_____

Paul is clear that we are saved by faith in God's grace which brings the Holy Spirit into our lives. That is how we continue to live as a Christian.

The Bible gives a very helpful illustration in *Romans 7 v 1–6.*

We are like a woman locked in a loveless marriage to Mr Law. This husband is unloving, very demanding, always right and never offers to help. Then, a death occurs. It is as though Mr Law dies, but actually we die to the law through Christ's death on the cross. We can now be married to a new husband, Jesus, who loves us and we love Him. We want to please Him and His approach is to help us to do what pleases Him.

Grace **makes us more holy** than the law did.

> 'Run John and live!' the law demands,
> But gives me neither legs nor arms.
> Better news the gospel brings,
> Bids me fly and gives me wings.'
> John Bunyan

Winning, Not Sinning

Some people think Christians are basically sinful. That's not true! We've been radically changed by the work of the Holy Spirit! The Bible says we are new creations. We have a **new heart** and a **new spirit**. People who are born again are basically righteous! Sin is out of character for the Christian!

John says,

'No-one who is born of God will continue to sin,
because God's seed remains in him;
he cannot go on sinningæ' *(1 John 3 v 9)*.

Indeed, John's reason for writing the letter was 'so that you will not sin'
(1 John 2 v 1).

John expected Christians not to sin, then he added:
'But, if anybody does sin...'

If we are foolish enough to sin, we can confess our sin and find mercy, but we don't **have to** sin in the first place.

It's a tragedy when Christians see themselves as basically sinners that will always be losing out to sin and temptation. The Bible says, 'We are more than conquerors .through Him who loved us' *(Romans 8 v 37)*

You are a **Conqueror**! A **Winner** not a sinner!

God has said to you, 'Be holy, because I am holy'.

📖 *Read 1 Peter 1 v 15–16.*

If you are fundamentally a sinner, you will have serious problems obeying this command. If an eagle says to a pig 'Fly because I fly' that pig is going to have a terrible identity crisis! If our hearts are basically sinful, how can we possibly be holy? The command is a recipe for disaster. It will ensure we are condemned and miserable.

But the truth is that if you are a Christian you **can** 'fly'.

God has given you His divine nature. He has called you to holiness and you have the capacity to be holy, to live like Jesus and be **'more than a conqueror'** through Him.

In *Romans 6 v 14* Paul says:
'sin shall not be your master'

This is not an exhortation; it is a statement of fact. By the saving power of God, when you were born again you were 'set free from sin and became a slave to righteousness' *(Romans 6 v 18)*. It is natural for righteous people to live righteously. Offer yourselves, then, as slaves of righteousness. When you live righteously you are being what **you are.**

The more you live for God and develop your relationship with Him, the more you'll find the inner leading of the Holy Spirit away from sin and towards holiness. One effect is you will find yourself uneasy about things you used to do and to say without a second thought!

Let yourself change!
Go with the inner promptings of the **Holy Spirit!**

Galatians 5 v 16 tells us that as we live following the Holy Spirit, we will simply no longer carry out our old sinful desires. The answer to the negative of sin is the positive of following after the Holy Spirit.

You will feel awful when you sin. That is good, it's a sign of your new master prodding you and saying 'Hey! What are you doing? Get back to doing the right thing!'. Tune in to your new master, Jesus. Love Him, talk to Him, get to know Him better and sin really won't be your master. You'll be 'filled with the fruit of righteousness that comes through Jesus Christ – to the glory and praise of God' *(Philippians 1 v 11).*

NOTES

UNIT

3

KINGDOM LIFE

The Kingdom Of God

Christians are people who have undergone a radical change. One way this is described in the Bible is in *Colossians 1 v 13–14.*

📖 ***Read Colossians 1 v 13–14 and fill in the blanks.***

'For He (God) has _____ us from the _____ of

_____ and brought us into the _____ of the

_____ He loves, in whom we have redemption, the forgiveness of sins.'

There are TWO spiritual kingdoms in this world:

» the dominion of darkness

» the kingdom of God

We all started off in the first one but,
we **WERE RESCUED** out of that and brought into God's kingdom
when we were born again by the Holy Spirit.

Jesus talked a lot about the kingdom of God.

📖 ***Look up these verses: Mark 1 v 15 and Matthew 4 v 23.***

The apostles also preached about the kingdom of God.

📖 ***Look up these verses: Acts 8 v 12 and Acts 28 v 31.***

A kingdom is a rule or government that affects your whole life.

| **Think About ...** | how being a citizen of the United Kingdom affects every aspect of your life. |

Tick everything in this list that is affected by being a citizen of the United Kingdom:

The language I speak ☐

The money I use ☐

Which side of the road I drive on ☐

When I had to start school ☐

How much tax I pay ☐

You should have ticked all of these and, of course, there are many other things that are affected by being a citizen of the United Kingdom.

As a Christian you now live under the government of King Jesus.
This also affects your **whole life.**

> You were once in the kingdom of darkness,
> under Satan's influence.
> Now you are in the kingdom of light
> under the rule of Jesus.

We have to learn how to live as citizens of the kingdom of God.

We do have someone to help us.

 Read Romans 14 v 17 and write down who it is who helps us to live like citizens of God's kingdom.

_____

Over the next four days we'll see how the Holy Spirit will help us to live as a citizen of God's kingdom in various different areas of life.

Kingdom Life – Personal

📖 *Read Ephesians 5 v 8-10 and then answer these questions:*

✍️ *How should we live? (v 8).*

_____

What are the main characteristics of the kingdom of light? (v 9).

1) _____ 2) _____ 3) _____

What is our main motivation in life now? (v 10).

_____

> Living under the rule of Jesus, in His kingdom, will affect our language

📖 *Read Ephesians 4 v 25; 29 and v 31.*

✍️ *Using your own words, list three ways of how living in God's kingdom will affect how you talk.*

1) _____ 2) _____

3) _____

Can you think of any ways in which your 'talk' has been affected by becoming a Christian?

> Being born again into God's kingdom will bring a radical alteration in our **attitude, actions** and **words** with regard to sex

📖 *Read Ephesians 5 v 3-5 carefully.*

This will be a battle ground because sexual immorality, impurity and obscenity are a huge part of the kingdom of darkness. Nevertheless, we will think, talk and act quite differently when we are under the leading of the Holy Spirit in the kingdom of God.

Something you will notice early on in your Christian life is a growing unease and a sensitivity of conscience about things you once thought nothing of. This is healthy and good. Follow after the Holy Spirit's leading and you will be changed into a good citizen in God's kingdom.

> *Ephesians 4 v 28* tells us of another radical area of change that happens when we become citizens of God's kingdom.
>
> **Stealing will stop!   Takers will become givers!**

Read Ephesians 5 v 17–20.

What is another 'kingdom of darkness' activity that will cease when we are in God's kingdom? (v 18).

_____

What is the positive that comes in to drive out the negative wrong behaviour? (v 18).

_____

We must remember that another way of describing kingdom life is:
'Spirit-filled Life'.

We are not under a new set of laws, but we live a life filled with the Holy Spirit and find that He will change every aspect of our lives.

In fact, you can't make rules for the Christian life because there are so many aspects to life that you would never make enough rules!

You	**WALK**	in the Holy Spirit
You	**LIVE**	to please God
You	**KEEP**	a clear conscience

If you maintain 'Righteousness, Peace and Joy in the Holy Spirit'
you won't go far wrong in daily life.

Kingdom Life – Family

With family life under constant attack in our day and standards falling in the world around us, our resources as Spirit-filled believers will enable us to be different and to follow the Word of God. God wants us to have **'Kingdom'** homes.

📖 *Read Ephesians 5 v 22–33.*

✏️ **List the attitudes and responsibilities of a husband in the kingdom of God.**

1) v 25 – _____

2) v 28 – _____

3) v 29 – _____

4) v 31 – _____

5) v 33 – _____

✏️ **List the attitudes and responsibilities of a wife in the kingdom of God.**

1) v 22 – _____

2) v 24 – _____

3) v 33 – _____

This study will probably lead to some lively **discussion!**

One thing to remember is this:

> » Husbands, let God speak to you about being a kingdom husband!

> » Wives, let God speak to you about being a kingdom wife!

And don't use the Bible to have a go at your partner!

NB *Ephesians 5 v 21* applies to every Christian, so our general attitude should ensure no exploitation, arrogance, manipulation or abuse in our relationships.

Ephesians 6 v 4 has some direct guidance for parents
(mothers and fathers can take heed to this!).

📖 **Read Ephesians 6 v 4 and also look at Colossians 3 v 21.**

God is the best child psychologist there is.
Parents take note of every word in these two verses.

All of us as children need to read prayerfully *Ephesians 6 v 1–3*. If you are adults, and, particularly if we are married, we need to balance these verses with *Ephesians 5 v 31*. When we marry we leave our parents to cleave to our partner. Direct obedience to parents applies to us in our pre-adult years, however, 'Honour your father and mother' always applies to us.

📖 **Read 1 Timothy 5 v 4 and v 8 for very practical teaching about good kingdom family attitudes.**

Being in the kingdom of God will change us whatever our age, sex or marital status.

📖 **Read Titus 2 v 1–6.**

> **Think** over which sentences might apply to you and
> **ask** the Holy Spirit to help you live a kingdom life.

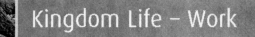

Kingdom Life – Work

Idleness is condemned in the Bible.

📖 *Read 2 Thessalonians 3 v 10–12.*

This passage refers to people who chose to be unemployed or made no effort to find work. They used spiritual arguments to excuse their idleness.

It is part of God's kingdom order that everyone should be active or busy *(v 11)*.

> » If you are unavoidably unemployed, **pray** that God will provide work for you
>
> » Then be prepared to take on any job that helps you to provide for yourself
>
> » While you are waiting for paid work, be prepared to keep busy with voluntary work that involves helping others

When we are in work, kingdom employees should be the best on the staff.

📖 *Read Ephesians 6 v 5–8.*

» don't just work for money but 'as if you were serving the Lord'
» be submissive and respectful to those in authority over you
» be honest and trustworthy

📖 *Read Luke 16 v 10–12 and notice:*

God's KINGDOM PROMOTION PRINCIPLES

» watch the small things
» handle money wisely
» treat other people's property with care

Kingdom bosses or employers should be the best to work for.

📖 *Read Ephesians 6 v 9 and Colossians 4 v 1.*

If you are in charge of people at work, remember you have a boss in heaven (Jesus) and behave in a way that would please Him. Be kind, fair, even-handed and generous to those under you.

Today ...

If you are unemployed	PRAY	for work and for God to guide you to use your time wisely
If you have a difficult boss	PRAY ASK	for him or her JESUS to help you see how you can be a better employee and let Jesus show you that you are serving HIM first and foremost
If you have difficult people under you at work	ASK	the Holy Spirit to help you to be LIKE JESUS in the way you treat them

NB This does not mean just being mild and tolerant!

Have another look at Jesus in the Gospels and get a balanced view.

You'll find Jesus very loving and patient but also courageous and confrontational when He met sin and hypocrisy in leaders who were responsible for people.

For example: *Luke 11 v 37–54 and Luke 19 v 45—20 v 8.*

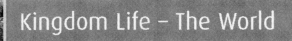

Kingdom Life – The World

All of us, whoever we are and whatever we do, need to have a right attitude as we live in this world. Remember we are surrounded by the kingdom of darkness, we shine as bright lights in a dark world.

Being a witness to Jesus is a lot more than just talking about God and church.

Read Matthew 5 v 13–16.

In Jesus' day, **'salt'** was used to stop things rotting. Christians are to hinder the spread of corruption **by their very presence** in society.

Jesus tells us **'light'** stands for our **'good deeds'** *(v 16)*. Our kingdom values which are different from those around us, are a very important part of our testimony. We are to earn the right to speak by the way we behave.

One of the ways we can be salt and light is to stay cheerful and not join in with the arguing and complaining that is all around us.

Read Philippians 2 v 14–16.

Always remember that this isn't a law. This is about letting the life of God **shine through you** (see *Philippians 2 v 13*).

Let God's Holy Spirit change you!

Read 1 Timothy 1 v 5.

Write down four elements that make up our **GOAL** in life:

1)   L _____

2)   P_____ H _____

3)   G _____ C _____

4)   S _____ F _____

Some Christians can be 'super-spiritual'. That means they try to talk in a religious way and make pious comments about everything.

Other Christians can be 'legalistic'. That means they live by a list of 'Do's and Don'ts'. They often get very judgmental of other Christians.

The right way to live is summed up in *1 Corinthians 10 v 31:*

> All that you do,
> EVERY DAY, ORDINARY THINGS,
> should be done
> TO GOD'S GLORY.

This means you should be able to **thank God** for everything and talk to Him about anything and everything you do.

If you can't thank Him and talk to Him it may be an indication you shouldn't be doing it! Also, you can be **in faith** that God is interested in **everything** you do and you can ask Him for help and provision about even the smallest thing.

We are to be **Supernaturally Natural &
Naturally Supernatural !**

Remember God is **for** you, not **against** you!

God wants you to be **ambassadors** for His kingdom of light in a world that is ruled by darkness. This is both a great privilege and a great challenge!

NOTES

4

KINGDOM
WARFARE

Know The Enemy

There is a major complication to the kingdom truth that we looked at in the last unit. It is that the kingdom of God and the dominion of darkness are at war!

Satan holds most of mankind under his influence. Sin has given him a legal hold over human beings. However, God has embarked on a rescue mission. He sent His Son, Jesus, to deal with our sin problem by His death on the cross. The kingdom of God has invaded Satan's territory and is bringing deliverance to the captives!

When we enter the kingdom of God, we enter a kingdom that is **at war** with Satan's kingdom. We join the army of God and we're on active service in enemy territory.

Ephesians 6 v 12 tells us something of the dominion of darkness that we are fighting against. A Christian is aware that there are **'spiritual forces of evil'** at work in this world and that our problems are often more than mere flesh and blood!

The devil, or Satan, is a real being who is a fallen angel.

Some of his names are:

Accuser *(Revelation 12 v 10)*	Serpent *(Genesis 3 v 1)*
Tempter *(Matthew 4 v 3)*	Angel of light *(2 Corinthians 11 v 14)*
Liar *(John 8 v 44)*	The evil one *(1 John 2 v 14)*
Murderer *(John 8 v 44)*	

Satan has a kingdom of fallen angels, or demons, that work with him. *(See Matthew 25 v 41).*

The devil is not equal with God, for example, he is not all-knowing or all-powerful. However, ever since Adam sold out to Satan in the Garden of Eden, the rulership of the world of men outside God has been under the power of the devil. He is sometimes called the **'god of this world'**. *See 1 John 5 v 19.*

Jesus had to withstand temptation from Satan.

 Read Luke 4 v 1–13 and notice how Jesus resists the devil by believing and speaking the Word of God.

We can be encouraged that Jesus understands what it's like to be in this sin-sick world and to be tempted by Satan. This same Jesus will help us in our fight with the evil one.

Notice that even the Lord's Prayer includes phrases about keeping us from the evil one and not being led into temptation and also prays for God's kingdom to come and His will to be done on earth as it is in heaven. So, you can see that kingdom warfare is at the very heart of Christianity.

Our Father in heaven, hallowed be your name,
Your kingdom come;
Your will be done on earth as it is in heaven.
Give us today our daily bread.
Forgive us our debts,
As we also have forgiven our debtors.
And lead us not into temptation
But deliver us from the evil one.

(Matthew 6 v 9–13)

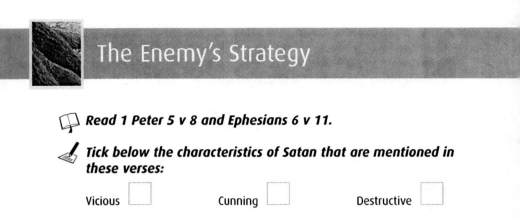

The Enemy's Strategy

📖 **Read 1 Peter 5 v 8 and Ephesians 6 v 11.**

✏️ **Tick below the characteristics of Satan that are mentioned in these verses:**

Vicious ☐ Cunning ☐ Destructive ☐

(You should have ticked all three!)

An enemy like this does not 'play fair' or 'give you a break'. He will choose times to attack that are most favourable for his evil plans to succeed. Remember, he tempted Jesus just after Jesus had been fasting for forty days and while he was in a hot wilderness.

Some of Satan's ways of attack are:

Zechariah 3 v 1	»	He accuses
2 Corinthians 11 v 14	»	He deceives
1 Thessalonians 3 v 5	»	He tempts
2 Corinthians 2 v 11	»	He tricks
2 Timothy 2 v 26	»	He traps
Luke 13 v 11, v16	»	He uses sickness
Hebrews 2 v 14–15	»	He uses fear

The Bible talks about strongholds.

📖 **Read 2 Corinthians 10 v 4–5.**

In the Old Testament a stronghold was a fortress where enemy troops could hold out and from where they could organise destructive raids on God's people.

Satan can have **'strongholds'** in our lives. They are built on areas of sin or, sometimes, areas of bondage from our pre-Christian days. Involvement in cults, drugs, sexual perversion, sexual promiscuity, alcoholism, idolatry, witchcraft and other occult practices can have formed strongholds in our lives.

2 Corinthians 10 v 5 shows us that a stronghold will involve **our thought life**. It will create an area of bondage in our thinking and in our behaviour that will cause us to constantly question God, contradict His Word and glorify sin and self.

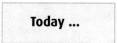

Today ...

Check your own areas of:

Doubt, Fear, Habitual sin.

ASK GOD to show you if these are normal struggles or demonic strongholds.

In the Kingdom of God you have all the grace you need to live in victory but, to do so, these strongholds need to be demolished. It is worth being open to God exposing areas of past sin or pain that could have formed demonic strongholds that need demolishing. Something similar was mentioned in Unit 2, Day 1. Usually, these strongholds are built on lies about God or ourselves. We need to know the **truth** of God's Word and the **power of His Spirit**. (John 8 v 32; Ephesians 6 v 17)

> *If you feel there are things that are not dealt with,*
> *talk to the person taking you through this course*
> *and be prepared for others to help you demolish*
> *any 'strongholds' in your life.*

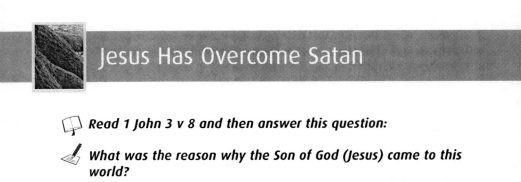

Jesus Has Overcome Satan

📖 *Read 1 John 3 v 8 and then answer this question:*

✏️ *What was the reason why the Son of God (Jesus) came to this world?*

_____

📖 *Read 1 John 4 v 4 and then answer these questions:*

✏️ *Who is 'the one who is in you'?* _____

✏️ *Who is 'the one who is in the world'?* _____

✏️ *Which 'one' is the greater?* _____

The decisive victory over Satan was won by Jesus on the cross.

📖 *Read Colossians 2 v 13–15.*

Your sins gave Satan a legal and real hold on your life. Jesus' death destroyed that ground from under Satan's feet. You are legally free by the blood of Jesus and you must learn to stand and fight on the ground Jesus has won for you.

📖 *Read Hebrews 2 v 14–15.*

Jesus died as a man on our behalf and, therefore, destroyed Satan's oppressive hold on our lives. We do not need to fear him anymore.

We can now live and act as Jesus did towards Satan:

📖 *Matthew 4 v 1–11.*
Resisting his temptations and deterring him with the Word of God.

📖 *Matthew 12 v 28*
Demonstrating the superior power of the Holy Spirit and the Kingdom of God.

Acts 10 v 38

Delivering those oppressed by the devil through sickness and evil.

Satan's final destiny has been decided. (*See Matthew 25 v 41.*) Although he still clings to power where men and women reject God and welcome sin, all the devil's fights are now fights of retreat!

How we Overcome Satan

We share in Jesus Christ's victory. We have to learn to fight with spiritual strategies and spiritual weapons. We are called to liberate men and women from the dominion of darkness and to see an extension of the kingdom of God on earth. We have both defensive and offensive battles to fight.

Here are some of the keys to gaining victory in spiritual warfare:

> » Recognise Satan's activities

📖 *Read 2 Corinthians 2 v 11.*

Don't be unaware of the devil's schemes. Schemes such as trapping us in unforgiving attitudes (2 Corinthians 2 v 10) or in bitterness and anger (Ephesians 4 v 26–27).

> » Find our the **truth** in God's Word which counteracts the devil's lies. Stand on that **truth**.

📖 *Read John 8 v 31–32.*

> » Reject the devil's attempts to get a foothold in your life

📖 *Read Ephesians 4 v 26–27.*

You do this by obeying the Holy Spirit's promptings and living 'kingdom of God' lifestyles.

> » Resist the devil's open and vicious attacks

📖 *Read 1 Peter 5 v 8–9.*

These are attempts to get you fearful and doubting and hurting. Open attacks are aimed at removing you from the battle. Sometimes we need the help of Christian friends to counter-attack in these days of direct assault by the evil one. Be encouraged that when we resist the devil we can expect him to eventually flee *(see James 4 v 7)*.

| » | Consciously stand on the **victory of Jesus** and declare your faith in Him |

📖 *Read Revelation 12 v 11 and Romans 10 v 8–10.*

Active faith has the Word of God in our hearts and in our mouths.

| » | Remember Jesus has given all **the authority** we need to deal with Satan and to see the kingdom of God advance |

📖 *Read Luke 10 v 19 and Matthew 28 v 18–20.*

| » | We can use **the Name of Jesus** against the enemy |

📖 *Read Mark 16 v 17–18.*

We can see an example of this in *Acts 16 v 18.*

| » | We have been provided with **spiritual armour** and **spiritual weapons** which we must use |

This is the subject of the next day's study.

Your Armour And Weapons

Today we will focus on one important passage of scripture.

📖 ***Read carefully Ephesians 6 v 10 –20.***

First of all, it is important to notice that we are not alone in this battle.

📖 ***Look at Ephesians 6 v 10 and fill in the blanks:***

✍️ *'Finally, be strong in the _____ and in His*

_____ _____.'

We are in Christ and Christ is in us by His Holy Spirit.

However, God has given us armour and weapons which we must **put on.**
The suggestion all through this passage is that **we have a responsibility** to put on or take up what God has provided.

The picture here is of a Roman soldier. So, let's use our imagination so as to fully understand what God is saying to us. This is our spiritual equipment:

1. The Belt of Truth
This would have held the soldier's tunic firm and tidy in battle so that he didn't stumble. It was also the fixing point for the armour and the sword's sheath.

For us the belt of truth is the **absolute truth of God's Word.** We buckle round ourselves clear, revealed truths that we find in God's Word.

2. The Breastplate of Righteousness
The breastplate protected the soldier heart and other vital organs.
Our breastplate is the **righteousness of Christ.** We protect our heart and emotions by being secure in the righteousness of Christ that is given to us.

3. The Gospel Boots (or Sandals)
Roman soldiers had well-fitted, spiked sandals to ensure they kept their footing in battle. Christians need to stand on **the Gospel** – their salvation through Jesus'

death and resurrection. This makes them sure footed in battle. We can add that it is with this that we advance into the world. It is the Gospel that we take to men and women around us.

4. The Shield of Faith
Roman shields were made to withstand flaming arrows and were large enough to protect the whole body. Our **faith** is an important part of our protection in spiritual warfare. We need to actively grasp and proclaim what we believe when Satan throws flaming arrows at us. By the way, although these are not physical arrows, they are **real** ones – real spiritual missiles hurled at us. If we do not use our shield of faith these missiles will hit the target and hurt.

5. The Helmet of Salvation
A helmet protects a soldier's head. A blow to the head can be fatal or render you unconscious. Satan wants us to be taken completely out of the battle. Therefore, he will attack our **minds**. We must protect our **thinking** by securing our minds with the full understanding of our salvation. This is why studies like this are so important. God wants your minds informed about your salvation.

6. The Sword of the Spirit
We're told that this is the **Word of God.** This is largely an offensive weapon. The Greek words here show us that the meaning is **the spoken Word of God**. We're talking about speaking God's Word in the power of the Holy Spirit in a way that is appropriate to a 'now' situation. The best example of this is Jesus dealing with the devil in *Matthew 4 v 1–11.*

We need to **know** God's Word. We need to **read** God's Word.

However, we also need to **speak** God's Word in faith if it is to be an effective weapon against Satan.

7. Prayer
This is not described as a specific weapon but it is mentioned five times in *Ephesians 6 vs 18–20.* Prayer is relevant to all the armour and weapons. It is our relationship with God that makes all the rest living and effective and **prayer** is the **heart** of our relationship with God.

Notice, we can pray on all occasions and with all kinds of prayers.
Prayer is talking to God as a friend and father, honestly and sincerely in any and every circumstance.

We are exhorted to always 'pray in the Spirit'.

The Holy Spirit helps us to get through to God *(see Ephesians 2 v 18).*

The Holy Spirit helps us in our weaknesses in prayer
(see Romans 8 v 26–27).

If we are going to be effective in prayer, we need to recognise our dependency on the Holy Spirit. We should **walk in the Spirit** every day, that means let Him lead us in our daily lives (see *Galatians 5 v 25).* We should go on continually being filled with the Holy Spirit *(Ephesians 5 v 18).*

The instructions to **walk in the Spirit** and go on **continually being filled with the Spirit** are both clear in our Bibles. An essential element of spiritual warfare is to be an actively, consciously, spirit-filled Christian!

Please talk to the person taking you through this course
about any issues raised by this study.

5

JESUS IS BUILDING HIS CHURCH

What Is The Church? (Part 1)

📖 *Read Matthew 16 v 13–18.*

Christianity is far more than just 'Jesus and me'. When Peter made his confession, Jesus didn't focus solely on Himself, He introduced **the church.**

When we confess Christ, God doesn't leave us to get on with things alone, He immediately brings us into His church.

However, mention 'church' to someone and you are almost guaranteed to get a negative response. Church is a cold, grey, stone building with pews and pulpits. It's boring services and a handful of elderly people. It's jumble sales and a 'restore the steeple' fund that's been running for ages. When Jesus said 'I will build my church', is this what He meant?

Never! The sort of church He planned was like the one in the New Testament – not statues and steeples, **but people and power!**

The New Testament church is Christians:

- » Loving and serving one another
- » Praising God and praying together
- » Prophesying and speaking in tongues
- » Healing the sick and bringing many to Christ

That's the church Jesus wants today.

📖 *Read these verses of the New Testament and then carefully read the statements made in the notes.*
Let God change your thinking about church.

1 Corinthians 1 v 2.
The church is not a building you go to but a **people you belong to**: people born again by the Holy Spirit who are committed to Jesus and to one another.

1 Corinthians 3 v 16.
The church is God's temple. God lives in and with His people by His Holy Spirit. If you want to meet God you don't go to a special building, you go to **gatherings of Spirit-filled Christians.**

Acts 2 v 47.

The church is not a club you opt to join, but **God's family** to which you are **'added'** by God Himself.

Acts 2 v 44–47.

The church is not to do with religious services, but with our **whole life together** in our homes and families.

Matthew 16 v 16–18.

The church is built by Jesus. The foundation is a **personal faith in Him** as Saviour and Lord, leading to a **personal relationship** with Him. There is no other way to belong to Jesus' church.

What Is The Church? (Part 2)

📖 *Look up these verses and fill in the word that is missing from each one:*

Galatians 6 v 10.

'Therefore, as we have opportunity, let us do good to all people,

especially to those who belong to the _____ of believers.'

Ephesians 3 v 14–15.

'For this reason I kneel before the Father, from whom His whole

_____ in heaven and on earth derives its name.'

Hebrews 2 v 11.

'Both the one who makes men holy and those who are made holy are of

the same _____. So, Jesus is not ashamed to call them brothers.'

✍️ *Write down in your own words why the family is such a good picture of the church:*

_____

_____

You already belong to the church. When you were born again Jesus brought you into **His worldwide family.**

Your new brothers and sisters come from all:
          races, tribes, languages, cultures, colours and classes.

They love Jesus and they are learning to love one another too.

You may ask, *'If I'm already in the church worldwide, why do I need to be in a local church too?'*. The simple answer is that you not only belong to God, you belong to others as well. If the church is a family, the members should be spending time enjoying one another's company.

God has given you a special job to do. Unless you join a **local church**, how will you do it? How will you use the gifts He's given you to build up other believers? How will you cope when things get tough and you need Christians to help and encourage you? We need Jesus and each other, so it is vital for us to meet together with other Christians.

Jesus expected his followers to work out their faith in the context of a local church.

Read Matthew 18 v 15–20.

In this short passage we can see the following things are important in Jesus' view of local church life:

- » Relationships – v 15

- » Structure – vs 16 and 17

- » Discipline – v 17

- » Authority – v 18

- » Prayer – v 19

- » Fellowship – v 20

Which Church?

Once you have decided to join a local church, which will it be?

If you are looking for the perfect church, you can give up now!

Christians may have been forgiven by Jesus but they still make mistakes. Even the New Testament church wasn't perfect, but it is the best model we have. Look for a church that fits the biblical pattern most closely. Here and in the next two studies we'll be looking at that pattern.

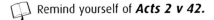 Remind yourself of **Acts 2 v 42.**

1) Apostles' Teaching
In a New Testament pattern church the **Bible will be central**. The early Christians studied their scriptures (Old Testament) and listened to the Apostles teaching about Jesus and how He wanted them to live. They carefully read the letters the Apostles wrote and lived out what they were learning. Those letters are now part of our New Testament.

A good church will believe that the **Bible is the Word of God**. In the preaching the speaker won't focus on his own ideas but on what God says. Many of the congregation will have Bibles open on their laps and some will be taking notes. You'll get the impression that they aren't just listening to the Word, but that they really want to live by it.

2) Fellowship
The New Testament Christians **loved each other** like members of a family. They **spent time** together and **shared meals.** They even sold their possessions to meet each others' needs *(Acts 4 v 32–35).*

A good church doesn't just have Sunday services. The members will meet during the week, probably in small home groups. As well as the organised meetings, members will see each other socially and informally. When one person is in need, others will offer practical help.

3) Breaking Of Bread
Jesus commands His followers to take bread and wine in memory of His death on the cross. The early church obeyed Him and broke bread in one another's homes.

In a biblical church, breaking bread isn't a formal and sombre Sunday occasion. It's a **celebration of Christ's love** which believers can enjoy in their homes as well as in large gatherings. While they'll remember Christ's sufferings they'll also recall His resurrection and look forward to His return.

 Read 1 Corinthians 11 v 23–29 then answer the following questions:

What do the bread and wine represent? (v 24–25).

_____

Until when do we break bread? (v 26).

_____

What should we do before we break bread? (v 28).

_____

4) Prayer

The New Testament believers prayed a lot, both alone and in groups. Why? Because God says that **if we pray, He will act.**

A good church will have a healthy prayer life. Look at the **prayer meetings.**

Are there many?
Are they well attended?
Are they lively?
Does prayer occur in several different settings?

Is it clear that prayer is an important part of this church's life?

Once you join a church you should be loyal and committed.
However, before you do join you have a duty to consider,
prayerfully and thoughtfully,
if the church you are joining is endeavouring to build
to a New Testament pattern.

A Worshipping Church

Today, we are continuing to consider the elements of a biblical church.

Worship should be a very important part of church life. You could argue that there is no higher calling than to be a people who worship the living God.
See *Isaiah 43 v 21* and *Ephesians 1 v 5–6 and v 11–12.*

📖 *Read Philippians 3 v 3 carefully.*

True believers worship by the Spirit, glory in Christ and put no confidence in the flesh.

 Don't join a church just because it has got a good Pastor or Youth Group.

 Join it because you know that the people worship by the Spirit.

📖 *Read John 4 v 21–24 and then answer this question:*

✎ *What is God the Father seeking in this time in which we live?*

NEW TESTAMENT WORSHIP IS:

Worship with Understanding	» We worship a God we **know**
Worship of the Father	» It is out of a **living relationship** with God, where we are born again by His Holy Spirit into His family and, therefore, become His children.
Worship in Spirit	» We are made **spiritually alive** by being born again. The Holy Spirit lives in us and helps us to worship God.
Worship in Truth	» We base our worship on the **truth** of what God is like and what He has done. This is rooted in what He has told us in His Word, the Bible. New Testament worship will be in **harmony with the Word of God.**

God wants you to be a worshipper.

Worship involves your mind, heart, body and will.

Your Mind	Read your Bible, let it influence your worship. Think about your prayers and the songs you sing. When you are worshipping use your mind.
Your Heart	Maybe you find it hard to express emotion. You like the spontaneous style of worship, but struggle with the idea of shouting to God with cries of joy *(Psalm 47 v 1)*. God wants you to overcome your reserve. He's worthy of lively, 'felt' praise and worship. Be open to the Holy Spirit touching and releasing your emotions.
Your Body	People in the Bible worshipped God by raising hands, singing, clapping, shouting, dancing, kneeling and even laughing. God wants you to do these things. Praise is enjoyable. Why not enjoy it?

Some biblical aspects of Praise & Worship.

» Lifting up hands *(Psalm 63 v 4; Psalm 134 v 2; 1 Timothy 2 v 8)*.

» Singing *(Psalm 33 v 1; Ephesians 5 v 19)*.

» Making Music *(Psalm 150 v 3-5)*.

» Dancing *(Psalm 150 v 4)*.

» Inexpressible Joy *(Psalm 126 v 1-3; 1 Peter 1 v 8)*.

Your Will	Worship is more than just praising God. It's about yielding to Him too. It's about saying, 'Lord, I'm going to do your will regardless of the cost'. God loves to hear that. It's the best expression of worship you can offer Him.

📖 *Read Romans 12 v 1-2.*

Remember, you must not only join a worshipping church, you must yourself **be a worshipper.**

A Member Of The Body

A very common New Testament picture of the church is that of a body.

📖 *Read Ephesians 4 v 15–16 and Colossians 2 v 19.*

Notice the **Head** of the body is Jesus Christ. Every part of the body needs a living link with the **Head.**

However, if I have a living link with Jesus and you do as well, then we have a living link with each other. We not only belong to Jesus Christ, **we belong to each other.**

📖 *Read Romans 12 v 4–5.*

We are now going to look at the most detailed passage in the New Testament about how the body of Christ works. We must apply this passage to our local church body.

📖 *Read 1 Corinthians 12 v 1–31.*

To be a biblical Christian in a New Testament church your lifestyle and experience must come somewhere near to this passage of Scripture.

Pray that God will lead you to a living, working, local body.

How to play your part as a member of the body

» Be filled with the Holy Spirit *(v 13).*

» Play your part without envying someone else's *(v 15–16).*

» Make room for others. Don't try to do everything. Appreciate those who can do some things better than you and receive their gifts to you *(v 17).*

» Get to know your place in the body *(v 18–20).*

» Admit your need of other people. The local church is your life-support system. Don't be so independent that you can't be helped or advised or corrected *(v 21).*

» Value other believers. Be devoted to one another. Honour one another. Encourage one another *(v 22–24)*.

» Care for the other members of the body *(v 25–26)*.

» Discover your spiritual gifts and use them *(v 27–31)*.

» Make 'love' your chief aim *(1 Corinthians 13 v 1–3)*. Spiritual gifts are not to prove we are charismatic but are God-given ways of loving others in the church and in the world.

NOTES

6

BELONGING TO A CHURCH

A Healthy Church (Part 1)

In most churches the best way of implementing the truths looked at in UNIT 5 is through **small groups.**

Nowadays churches have a variety of names for these small groups e.g. Cell Groups, Community Groups, Life Groups, House Groups etc. Whatever the name, it is essential that the small groups are **'holistic'**. An 'holistic' small group is much more than a Bible Study group.

HOLISTIC SMALL GROUPS ARE GROUPS WHERE:

 » The Word of God is applied to daily lives.
 » Issues of life are shared and prayed for.
 » Relationships are formed.
 » Christians learn to serve others both inside and outside the group.
 » People learn to exercise their spiritual gifts.
 » The development of leaders is a product of normal group life.
 » Discipleship takes place that is practical and attainable.
 » There is a goal of growth and multiplication of the group.
 » Relational evangelism is encouraged.

These groups are places where ordinary Christians can pray for one another, encourage one another and build one another up.

NB The words **'one another'** or **'each other'** occur over 100 times in New Testament teaching to Christians. Here is a selection of some 'one another' verses. Read them and then write your own comments on what you have learnt from them:

Hebrews 3 v 13; 10 v 24–25; 1 Thessalonians 5 v 11; Colossians 3 v 13–16; Romans 12 v 10 and v 16; 15 v 7 and v 14; Galatians 5 v 13; 6 v 2; Ephesians 4 v 2 and v 32; James 5 v 16; 1 Peter 4 v 9

Comments:

_____

_____

_____

_____

_____

_____

Small groups will generally meet in homes, usually on a midweek evening, when they will often study the Bible and worship together.

However, a healthy small group is much more than a meeting a week. It is a living unit of the church intended for building each other up in the 3 great Commandments of Jesus.

📖 *Love for God* **(Matthew 22 v 37)**

📖 *Love for one another* **(John 13 v 34)**

📖 *Love for the world* **(Matthew 22 v 39)**

Obviously the midweek meeting is a key part of this and the meeting structure will reflect these 3 Commandments. All members of this church are encouraged to attend their small group meeting every week if at all possible.

This is not a burden but a joy as you begin to see how this will bless you and build you up.

Every member is expected to contribute to the life of the small group although the group will have a leader and an assistant or trainee leaders.

Many of you doing this course will already be involved in a small group and know what a benefit it can be in your Christian growth.

A Healthy Church (Part 2)

Small groups are a vital and non-negotiable part of church life but the church is more than a loose connection of small groups.

For a healthy bird to fly it needs two wings. For a healthy church to progress and 'fly with God' it needs two wings!

1 – small group wing; **2** – large group wing.

The **'large group wing'** is seen in our Sunday morning celebrations. The celebration lasts for approximately two hours and there are provisions for children and young people. This meeting is an essential part of church life. On Sunday morning we worship together in union with the whole church. We hear the Word of God preached by the Elders. We meet God in each other and in the dynamic of the whole body gathering as one. These are often powerful times when God speaks to us and people get saved and healed.

In fact the **'large wing'** is more than Sunday mornings. There will also be church prayer meetings and other social and spiritual gatherings.

The Church is structured something like this:

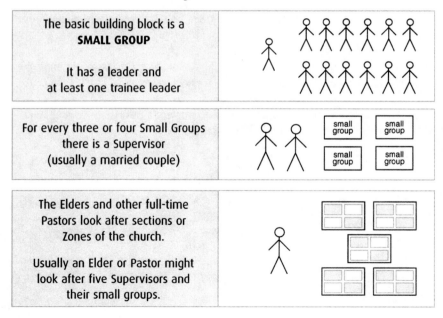

The basic building block is a **SMALL GROUP** It has a leader and at least one trainee leader	
For every three or four Small Groups there is a Supervisor (usually a married couple)	
The Elders and other full-time Pastors look after sections or Zones of the church. Usually an Elder or Pastor might look after five Supervisors and their small groups.	

In addition to this there will be administration staff, children's workers, musicians, youth leaders and a host of other volunteers doing practical work in the church. **BUT** they all belong to a small group.

We endeavour to ensure that the activities of the large group and the small groups do not compete but work together to make a strong, healthy church that progresses in the purposes of God.

Leadership

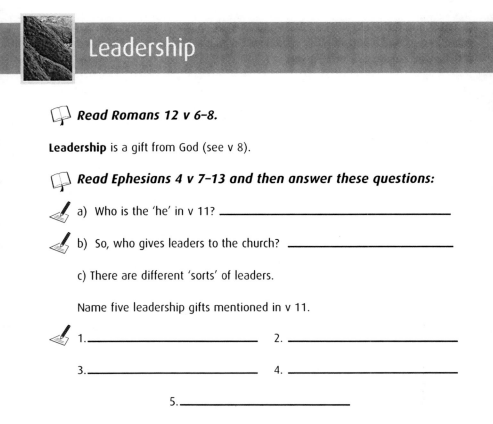

📖 ***Read Romans 12 v 6–8.***

Leadership is a gift from God (see v 8).

📖 ***Read Ephesians 4 v 7–13 and then answer these questions:***

a) Who is the 'he' in v 11? _____

b) So, who gives leaders to the church? _____

c) There are different 'sorts' of leaders.

Name five leadership gifts mentioned in v 11.

1._____   2. _____

3._____   4. _____

5._____

There are varieties of gifts in the church and no one person has all the gifts. Church leadership should be a **team** or **group** wherever possible.

The person taking you through this course can give you more details about how **Elders** are appointed in this Church. The **Elders** are the spiritual leaders of the Church and the following study applies primarily to your relationship with them.

For more biblical information on **Elders** see *1 Timothy 3 v 1–7* and *Titus 1 v 5–9.*

What should you expect of your leaders?

📖 ***Read Hebrews 13 v 7 and v 17:***

Fill in the blanks below:

They speak _____ to you.

You should want to imitate their _____.

They keep _____ over you.

They will have to give an _____ (to God).

📖 Read 1 Peter 5 v 2-3

They are to be _____ of God's flock.

They are to _____ as overseers.

They are not to be greedy for _____.

They are not to _____ it over those entrusted to them.

What does Jesus expect of you with regard to your leaders?

📖 Read Hebrews 13 v 7

_____ the outcome of their way of life.

_____ their faith.

📖 Read Hebrews 13 v 17 and 18.

_____ your leaders.

_____ to their authority.

Make their work a _____ not a _____.

_____ for us. (This is written by a leader)

📖 Read Hebrews 13 v 24.

_____ all your leaders.

If all **leaders** and all **church members** take heed to the relevant Scriptures we'll have a happy and united church.

These Scriptures apply to any Christian church and you should prayerfully consider them before joining a local church.

Stewardship (Part 1)

In the New Testament, being a Christian affected people's attitude to money right from the start.

 *Read Acts 2 v 45 and Acts 4 v 33–35.*

Our giving is part of our worship to God.

Read Deuteronomy 16 v 16–17.

Gifts and offerings are mostly collected on Sunday mornings during celebration meetings.

When you give to God – WHERE do you give?

Biblical giving is directed in two ways:

For those serving God and benefiting the church spiritually	*Read 1 Corinthians 9 v 7–11 and v 14. 1 Timothy 5 v 17–18.*
To relieve needs within the Christian community	*Read Acts 4 v 34–35. Romans 15 v 26.*

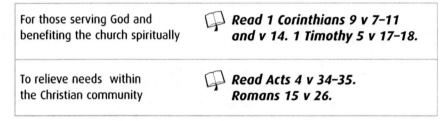

When you give to God – HOW MUCH do you give?

This is entirely up to you. You don't **have** to give anything. Your salvation is free and all of God's grace. Your giving **must** be a free will offering of thanksgiving to God.

Read 1 Corinthians 16 v 1–2.

This passage suggests our giving should be **planned** and **proportional** to our income. There is a biblical guideline for the proportion we should aim at. It is called the **'tithe'** i.e. giving God 10 % of what we receive as income. Everything we have belongs to God, we are just stewards of it. Tithing reflects our gratitude to God and our faith in Him as our provider.

Tithing was set in the law of Moses but it pre-dates Moses. Abraham, the father of those justified by faith (i.e. us!), tithed to Melchizedek, God's priest.
See Genesis 14 v 18–20.

Notice that Jesus never told us not to tithe but rather put His emphasis on the attitude in which we should tithe and give – more on that tomorrow!

Stewardship (Part 2)

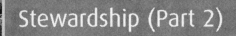

When you give to God – HOW should you give?

📖 *Read 2 Corinthians 9 v 6–8.*

2 Corinthians 9 v 6 – Give generously.
2 Corinthians 9 v 7 – Give freely.
2 Corinthians 9 v 7 – Give cheerfully.
2 Corinthians 9 v 8 – Give expectantly.

Throughout Scripture there is an important principle: **give in faith expecting God to generously meet all your own financial needs.**

Please read all the following Scriptures carefully and let God show you this principle. Then let faith arise for God's provision for you!

📖 *Proverbs 3 v 9–10.*   📖 *Malachi 3 v 8–10.*

📖 *Matthew 6 v 25–33.*   📖 *Luke 6 v 38.*

📖 *2 Corinthians 9 v 6–11.*   📖 *Philippians 4 v 15–19.*

Practical points :
We trust that, as a new member, you will join the church in giving financially out of gratitude to God, and in order to extend the Kingdom of God in the local area. The Church, in turn, always gives away at least a tenth of its income to a variety of needs and projects.

» Apart from the normal collection taken on Sunday morning, we occasionally have Gift Days for a particular need.

» Standing order payments are a great convenience to us. Please contact the Church Office staff for details or speak to a Church Leader.

» If you are a taxpayer, because this church is a registered charity, you can 'Gift Aid' your giving. This is very beneficial to us at no extra cost to you.

'Gift Aid' forms are available – please ask for one from a Church leader or the Church Office.

UNIT

7

SHARING
YOUR FAITH

You Will Be My Witnesses

📖 *Read Mark 5 v 18 –20.*

When Jesus set this man free, he was so grateful that he went off and told everyone what Jesus had done for him.

This is what it means to be a **witness** – you understand what Jesus has done for you and you cannot keep quiet. No one is forcing you to speak, you are so grateful to Jesus that you cannot help it!

People may ignore you or laugh at you and say you are going through a phase, but they cannot deny the reality of what you have.

📖 *Look at 2 Corinthians 5 v 17–21.*

✎ *What message do we have?*

_____ *(v 19)*.

✎ *What are we?*

_____ *(v 20)*.

✎ *How should we speak to people?*

_____ *(v 20)*.

📖 *Also look at 2 Corinthians 5 v 11 and 14.*

✎ *What drives us on?*

_____ *(v 14)*.

You may get your words muddled and your theology wrong. You may get stuck when people ask questions. Don't worry. Jesus doesn't expect you to know it all. Just say what He has done and let His love shine through you.

Giving a personal testimony (story)

A **personal testimony (story)s** comes over more powerfully if you know it well. Think about the following headings and then write down what you would say under each:

> **Where I was**

> **What the central focus of my life was before I was saved**

> **What happened**

> **Why I decided to become a Christian**

> **Where I am now**

> **The most important thing Jesus has done for me**

Practise your testimony with a friend until you can present it naturally and clearly in a few minutes.

Jesus was a **'friend of sinners'** (Matthew 11 v 19). He accepted people as they were and He took an interest in them. When people see you as their friend, they will listen to you. Relate to them; talk about ordinary things; don't pry; be friendly; let the love of Christ motivate you, not any desire to win an argument.

Actions Speak!

Our witness is not just words, it is **actions** too.

📖 *Read Matthew 5 v 14–16.*

✍️ *What will people do when they see our good deeds?*

_____ *(v 16).*

Often people are more impressed by what **we do** than what **we say**. Let them know what's happening to you but don't keep badgering them. Just live a new life. Be kind and helpful to them. Pray for them and speak when Jesus gives you the opportunity.

📖 *Read 1 Peter 3 v 13–17.*

We can expect opposition as we stand up for what is right and share about Jesus.

✍️ *What should we always be?*

_____ *(v 15).*

✍️ *How should we share the good news?*

_____ *(v 15 and 16).*

If people aren't interested in Jesus, don't argue with them or become discouraged. Be polite and let them believe what they want. They may ask you questions later. Concentrate on speaking to people who want to listen to you. God will honour you and one day He'll give you the joy of leading someone to Christ.

Be careful how you speak:

> *Ecclesiastes 10 v 12.*   *Luke 4 v 22.*
> *Ephesians 4 v 29.*   *Colossians 4 v 6.*

Leading Someone To Christ

Whether it is in a private conversation, at home or at work, whether it is in the small group or a big celebration meeting, someone, sometime, will ask you how to become a Christian.

Here are some verses to read and remember (maybe you should write them on the inside cover of your Bible) so that you can take a person through the steps to salvation:

The Problem:		
Sin separates	*Isaiah 53 v 6;*	*Isaiah 59 v 2.*
Sin's penalty	*Romans 3 v 23;*	*Romans 6 v 23.*
God's Answer:		
Jesus died for us	*1 Peter 2 v 24;*	*1 Peter 3 v 18.*
Our Response:		
Repent	*Acts 2 v 38;*	*Acts 3 v 19.*
Believe and Receive	*John 1 v 12;*	*John 3 v 16.*

Be prepared to lead your friend to Christ. If they are ready, encourage them to pray aloud. They can use their own words or follow you. Don't be afraid to guide or prompt, they will probably have never prayed aloud before!

Make sure they:

» Repent and renounce sin   (be specific if necessary)

» Thank Jesus for dying for them

» Ask for forgiveness and cleansing

» Invite Jesus into their life to be Lord, Master and Friend

Make sure they get linked up to a church where they will be looked after in their Christian life.

Encourage them to read the Bible, pray and be led by the Holy Spirit.

Pray for them yourself.

If possible, take them along to your small group, introduce them to the group leader and ask about any new-Christian materials which you could go through with them.

Signs And Wonders

📖 *Read Luke 4 v 18–19.*

How did Jesus see His mission?

✎ to preach _____

✎ to proclaim _____

✎ and _____

✎ to release _____

✎ to proclaim _____

📖 *Read John 20 v 21.*

Jesus sends us out as He was sent – to preach, heal and deliver.

What Jesus began, He wanted His disciples to continue.
See Luke 9 v 1–2; Luke 10 v 9; Mark 16 v 15–18.

If you are a believer in Jesus, then He has sent you to tell others about Him and to perform the signs of the Kingdom of God.

Some Christians are called to a ministry of signs and wonders. You may, or may not, be one of them – God will reveal this to you in His time. What He wants you to do now is to reach out to others whenever you get the opportunity.

Don't be frightened to move out in faith. Of course, you will need to be sensitive. Do they want you to pray for them? Do they mind if you put a hand on their shoulder?

If you are not of the same sex as the other person, take with you a Christian who is.

God may heal the people you pray for, but if He doesn't, don't be discouraged. You've asked God to bless someone. He or she is probably amazed that you care that much about them and they may well be willing to hear more about Jesus later. Remember you can't predict how God will answer. Some healing is gradual. You just keep reaching out and leaving the outcome in God's hands – it is what you've been sent to do.

Read and pray over Acts 4 v 29 and 30;
1 Thessalonians 1 v 5; John 14 v 12–14.

To The Ends Of The Earth

 *Read Isaiah 52 v 10.*

God has always had a definite goal: to win **a people for His Son** from all the **nations of the world.** Jesus knew He wasn't on the planet merely to reach a few individuals. He was here to win the world, whatever it cost Him. Jesus wanted His disciples to catch this vision. See *Acts 1 v 8.*

Read Luke 24 v 45–49.

What was the message to be preached to all nations?

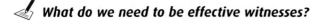 _____ *(v 46–47).*

What do we need to be effective witnesses?

_____ *(v 49).*

Once the disciples had received the Holy Spirit at Pentecost there was no stopping them. Burning in their hearts was **a passion to reach the nations for Jesus.**

So they preached the gospel everywhere and within twenty years they had touched the known world of their day.

It's easy to miss God's goal. God is changing you and blessing you. It's tempting to forget that there is a world out there that God wants you to reach. God blesses us so that we can bless others. We have the only answer for people everywhere.

God is after a people for His Son. He has a heart for every tribe, nation and tongue. You are part of a great army that God is raising up and mobilising to reach the world. Our mission is to the **whole world!**

Read and pray over:
Matthew 24 v 14.
Matthew 28 v 18–20.
Mark 16 v 15.
John 3 v 16.

The person taking you through this course will tell you about this church's main evangelistic strategies and involvement in mission projects at home and abroad.

NOTES

NOTES

NOTES

NOTES

NOTES

NOTES

NOTES

NOTES

NOTES

NOTES

NOTES

CPSIA information can be obtained
at www.ICGtesting.com
Printed in the USA
FFOW05n2006020315